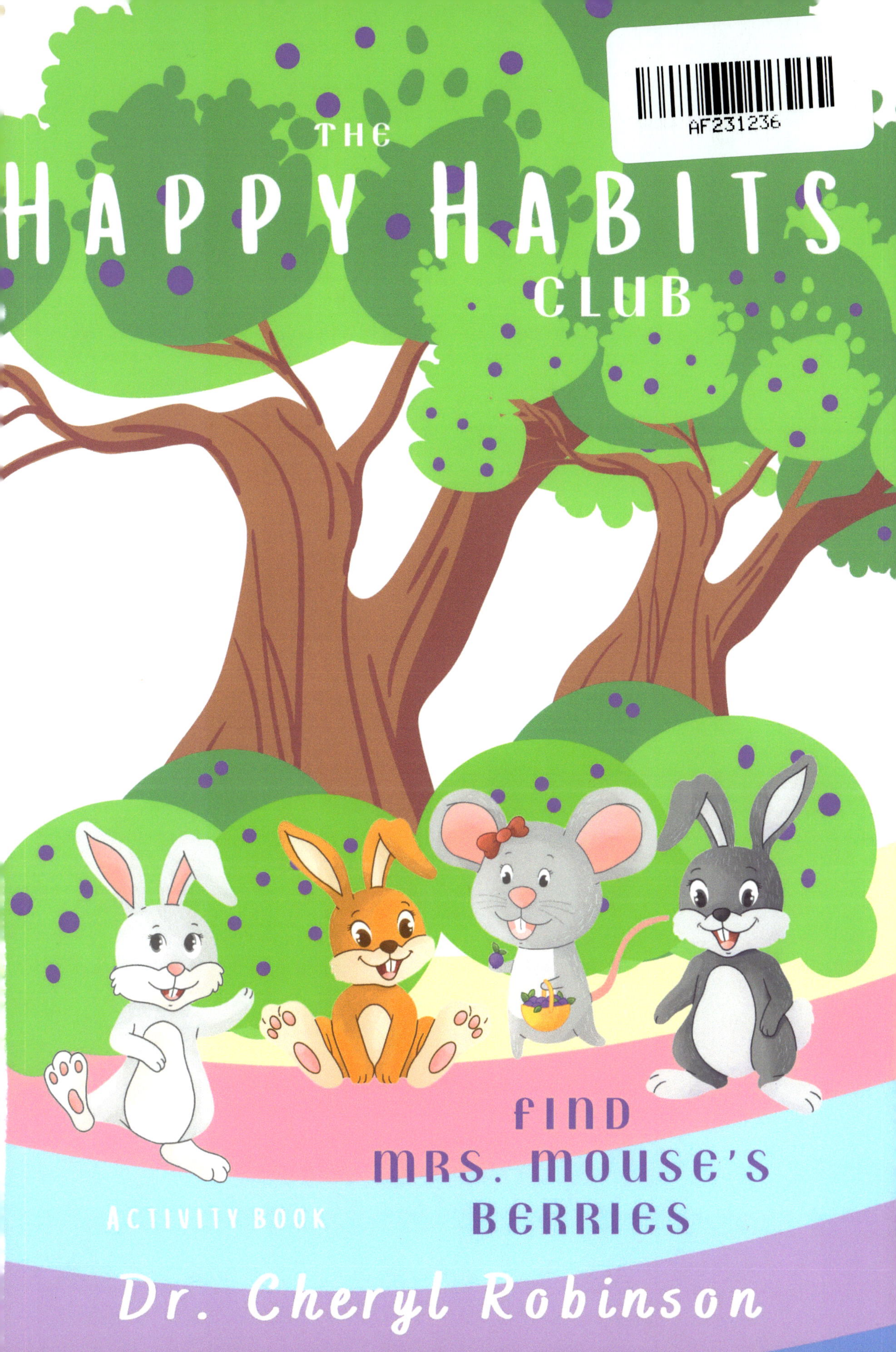

THE
HAPPY HABITS
CLUB
AF231236
FIND
MRS. MOUSE'S
BERRIES
ACTIVITY BOOK
Dr. Cheryl Robinson

Illustrations are used under the permitted licensing agreement from Canva pro membership 2023.

Thank you to the amazing illustrators for sharing your creativity:

Berries: @ed-cain,
Bees: from pixabay @miatroyleekho,
Deer: @ellettelorelei, Treehouse: @matthew-coles-images/@bnpdesignstudio, Sloth: from pixaby @ralphdesign, Lion: Изображения пользователя Svetlanarto, Giraffe: @sketchify, Ant: @thidaratsuteeratatphotos, Bluebird: @from TwaN's Images

Main characters illustrated by Ayu Putri

Creative Renegade Media
New Jersey

ISBN: 978-0-9856849-5-2

thehappyhabits.club

Dedication:

To my first love bug, Linds. You made me an aunt and have shown me the world through a different lens. Never let anyone dim your sparkle. Your light is bright, and you can accomplish whatever you put your mind to in this life. Love you to the moon and back, kiddo. Auntie Cher will always be in your corner.

There is a magical forest.
Home to sassy squirrels.
Busy bees.
Dandy deer.
And the Happy Habits rabbits.

Sisters Flip, Flop and Flo like to hip.

They like to hop. They dip fast.

They skip quick.

They have a secret club.
To help others find their happy.

No member is too small.
Too big.
Too loud.
Too quiet.
All are welcome to join.

"We're the happy habits rabbits.
We help turn frowns upside down.
Join us on our adventures.
We'll be your teachers.
We can make the forest feel good.
Do you think you could?
Bring your glow.
Let's go!"

Flip, Flop and Flo hipped and hopped.
They dipped and skipped around
the magical forest.

The three sisters ran
into Mrs. Mouse.

"We're the happy habits rabbits.
We help turn frowns upside down.
We hip. We hop. We dip. We skip.
Tell us why you are sad.
We will help you be glad."

"I was looking for berries.
To bring to Gerry's.
He ate a nut with mold.
Now, he has a cold.
I found berries under a tree.
But then I got stung by a bee.
My basket of berries spilled.
And berries rolled all over the hill."

"We're sorry to hear of your troubles.
We'll help you on the double.
We'll search high and low.
Even in the snow.
We're here to help you,
So you feel less blue."

Mrs. Mouse's berries
rolled everywhere.

Flip skipped to a
nearby tree.

Where she a met a
scared centipede.

"Hi, I'm Flip.
I'm happy when I skip.
I see you're scared.
I really do care.
Tell me why you are sad.
I will help you be glad."

"I was walking along,
Singing a song.
The ground started to rumble.
I began to stumble.
Berries rolled everywhere.
It gave me a scare."

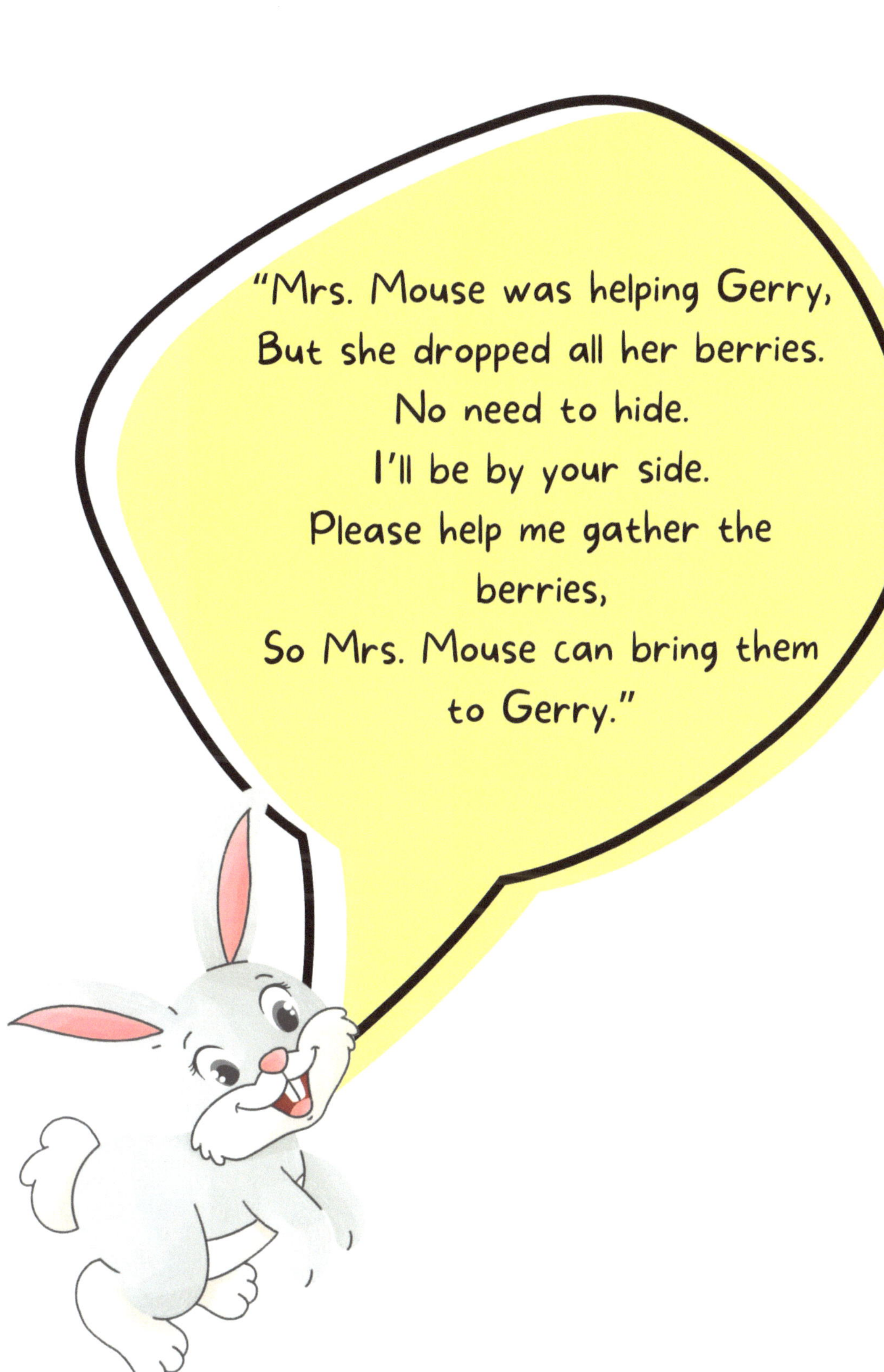

"Mrs. Mouse was helping Gerry,
But she dropped all her berries.
No need to hide.
I'll be by your side.
Please help me gather the berries,
So Mrs. Mouse can bring them to Gerry."

The centipede felt at peace.
He helped Flip gather the runaway berries.

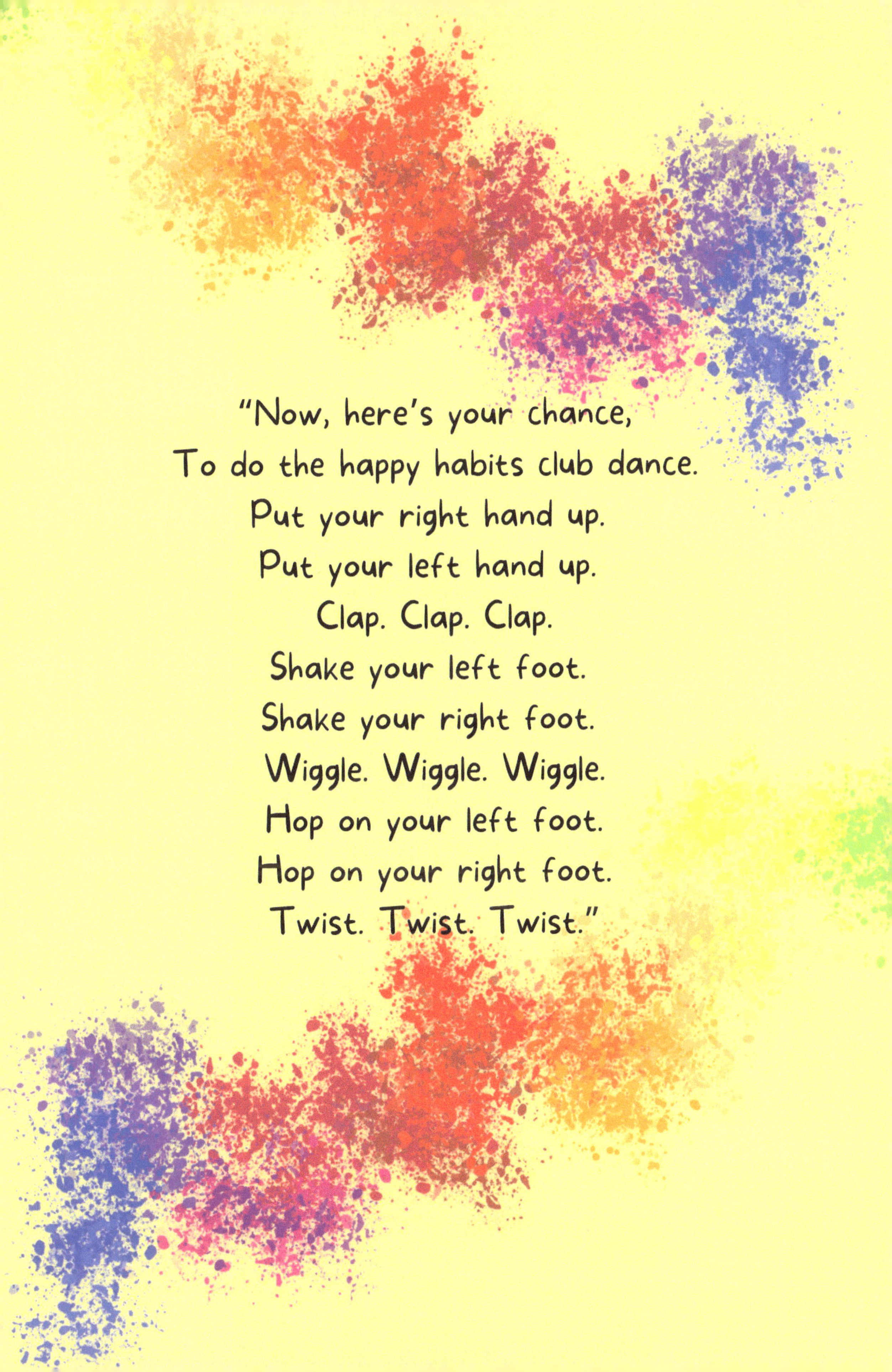

"Now, here's your chance,
To do the happy habits club dance.
Put your right hand up.
Put your left hand up.
Clap. Clap. Clap.
Shake your left foot.
Shake your right foot.
Wiggle. Wiggle. Wiggle.
Hop on your left foot.
Hop on your right foot.
Twist. Twist. Twist."

Clap
Wiggle
Twist

Flop hopped by the river.
She saw a silly beaver.

"Hi, I'm Flop.
I'm happy when I hop.
I see you have the giggles.
You're running in squiggles.
What are you laughing at?
Let's have a chat."

"I was building my dam.
When I had to scram.
Berries were falling from the sky.
One almost hit me in the eye.
I thought it would be fun,
If I ate one.
Now my tongue is blue.
And the water turned to goo."

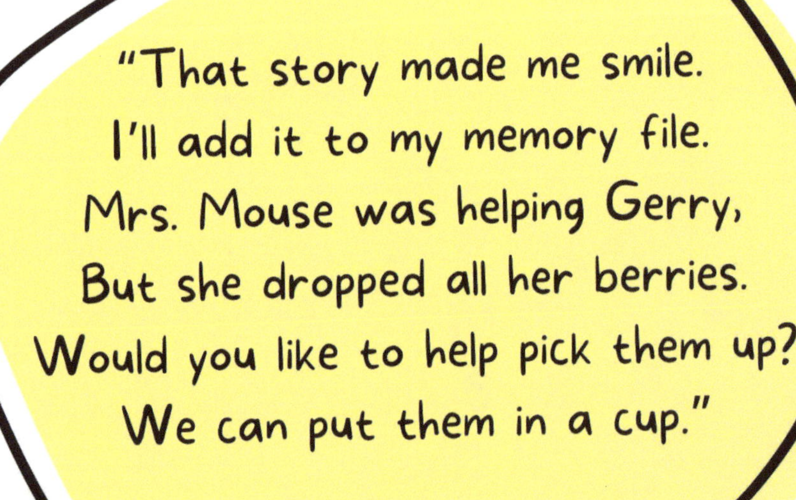

"That story made me smile.
I'll add it to my memory file.
Mrs. Mouse was helping Gerry,
But she dropped all her berries.
Would you like to help pick them up?
We can put them in a cup."

The beaver made Flop laugh.
The two new friends picked up
all the berries they could see.

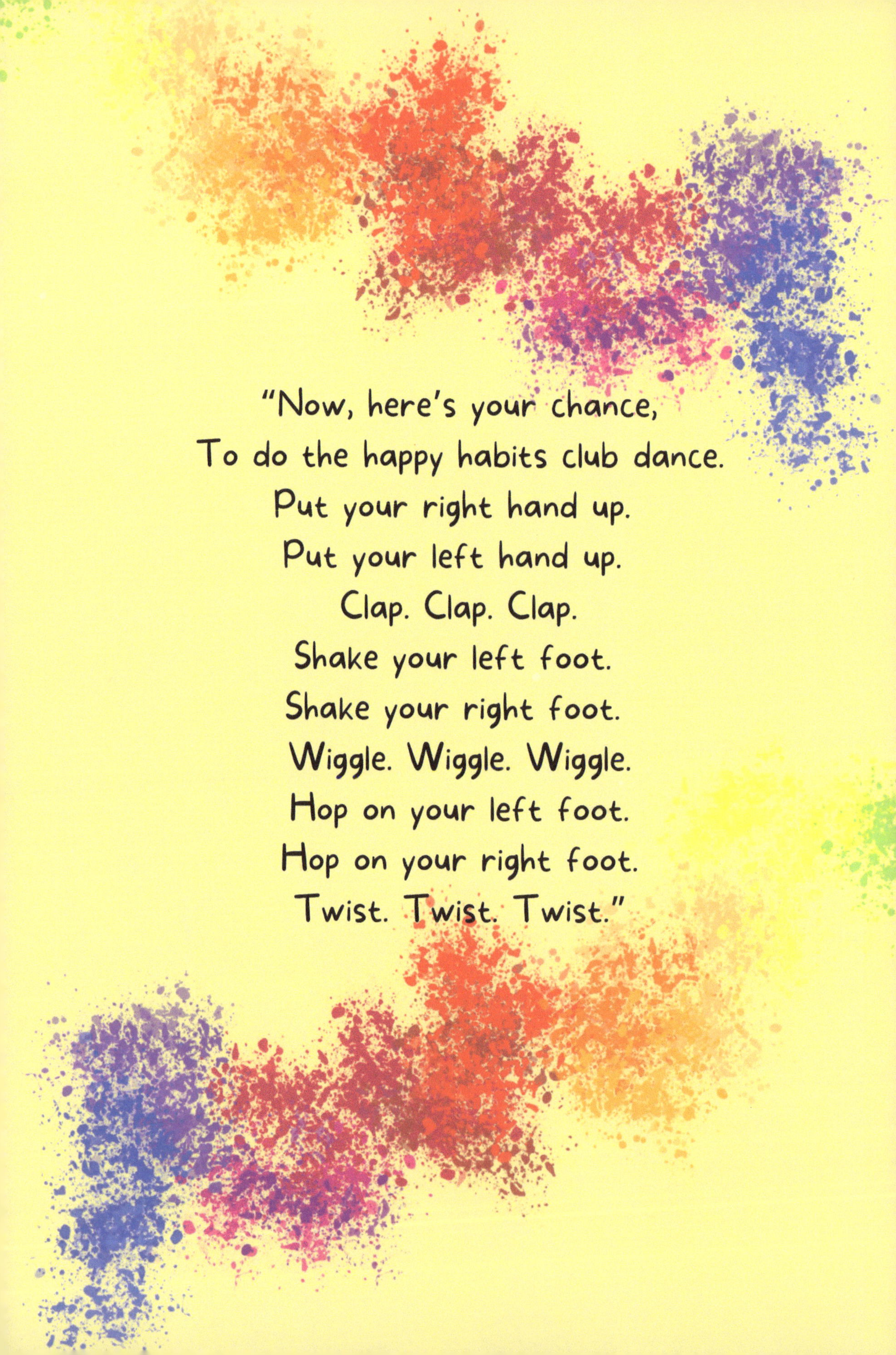

"Now, here's your chance,
To do the happy habits club dance.
Put your right hand up.
Put your left hand up.
Clap. Clap. Clap.
Shake your left foot.
Shake your right foot.
Wiggle. Wiggle. Wiggle.
Hop on your left foot.
Hop on your right foot.
Twist. Twist. Twist."

Clap

Wiggle

Twist

Flo hipped to the flowers.
She bumped into a tired raccoon.

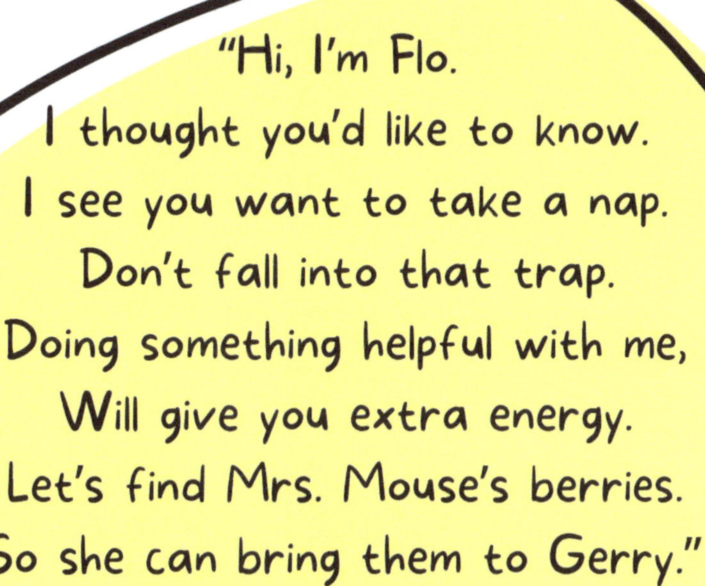

"Hi, I'm Flo.
I thought you'd like to know.
I see you want to take a nap.
Don't fall into that trap.
Doing something helpful with me,
Will give you extra energy.
Let's find Mrs. Mouse's berries.
So she can bring them to Gerry."

The raccoon helped Flo.
They gathered all the berries.

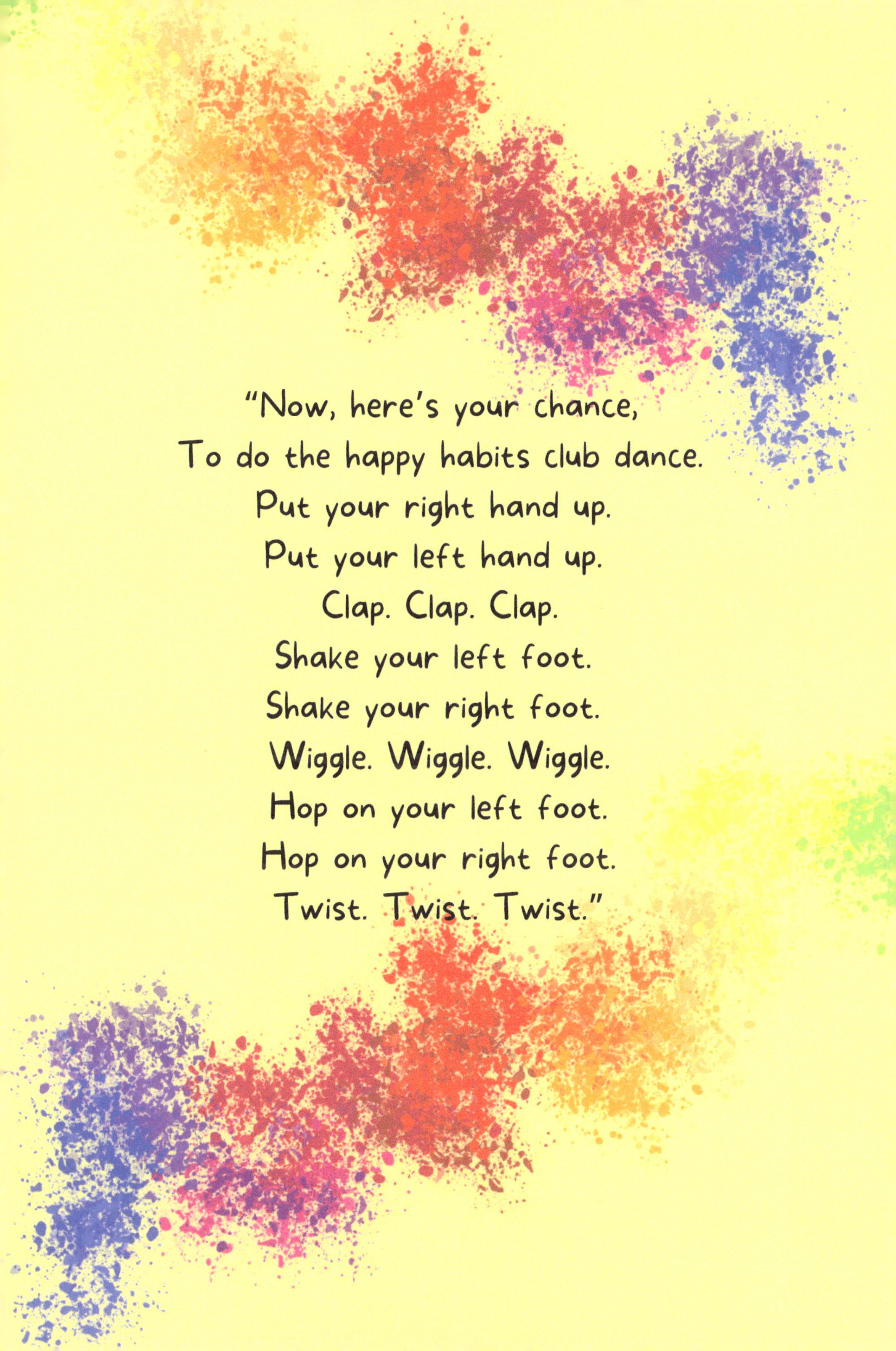

"Now, here's your chance,
To do the happy habits club dance.
Put your right hand up.
Put your left hand up.
Clap. Clap. Clap.
Shake your left foot.
Shake your right foot.
Wiggle. Wiggle. Wiggle.
Hop on your left foot.
Hop on your right foot.
Twist. Twist. Twist."

Clap
Wiggle
Twist

Flip, Flop, Flo and their friends took
the berries to Mrs. Mouse.

"Mrs. Mouse. Mrs. Mouse.
Let's go to Gerry's house.
We picked up all the berries.
And even added some cherries.
This will make him feel better.
We can even write a letter."

Dear Mr. Gerry,

Here are your berries.
Feel better soon.
So you can sing a happy tune.

-Your Happy Habits Club Friends

Once again, the happy habits rabbits
helped others find their happy.

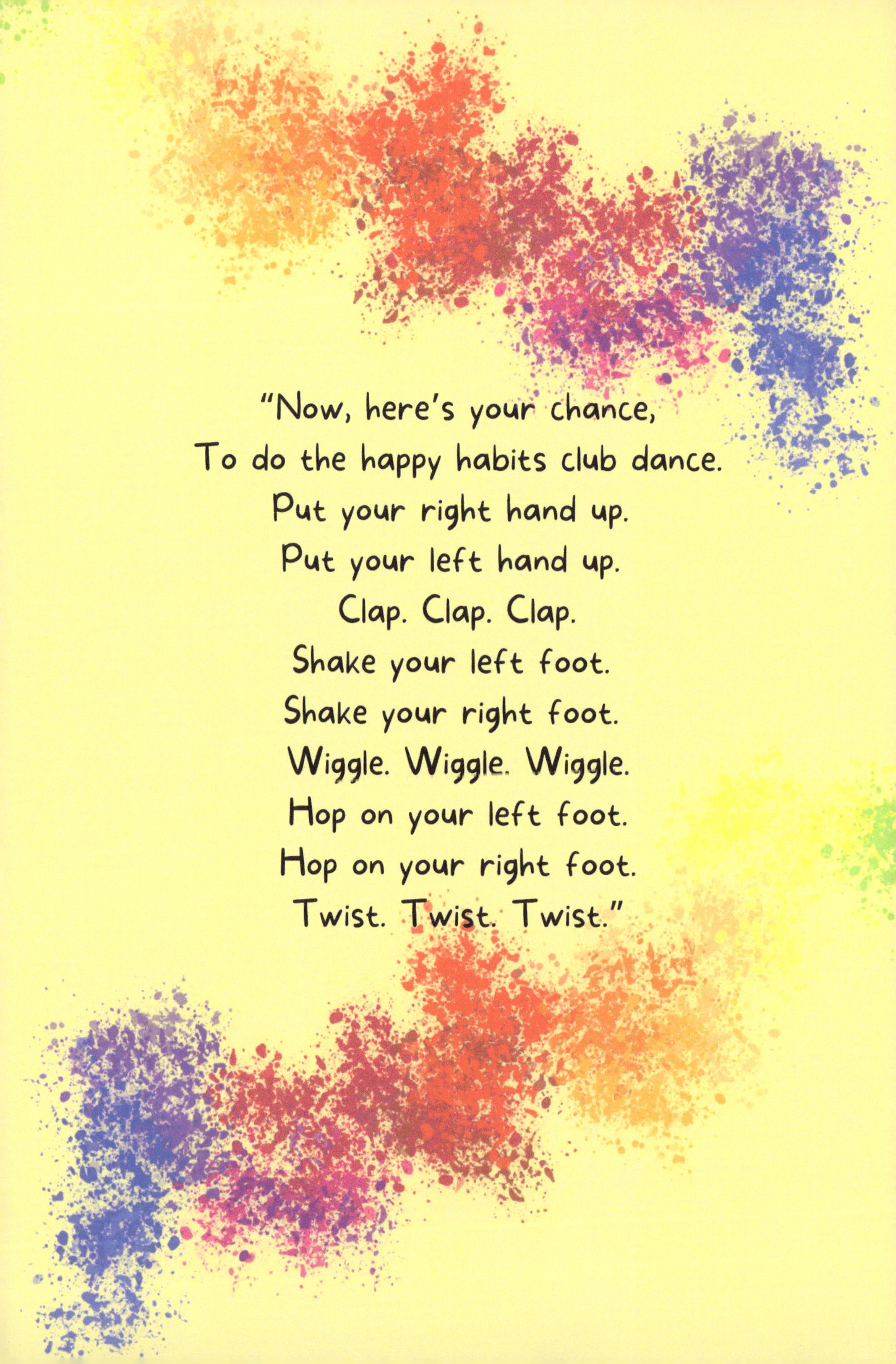

"Now, here's your chance,
To do the happy habits club dance.
Put your right hand up.
Put your left hand up.
Clap. Clap. Clap.
Shake your left foot.
Shake your right foot.
Wiggle. Wiggle. Wiggle.
Hop on your left foot.
Hop on your right foot.
Twist. Twist. Twist."

Clap
Wiggle
Twist

Certificate of Membership

Flip, Flop & Flo are excited to announce that

is now a member of the

Happy Habits Club!

Clap! Clap! Clap! Wiggle! Wiggle! Wiggle!

Welcome to the
Happy Habits Club!

Now that you're a member,
you can get started creating
Happy Habits!

The Happy Habits Tracker

- ◯ I played with an old toy
- ◯ I danced to my favorite song
- ◯ I made someone laugh today
- ◯ I helped cook dinner
- ◯ I dressed myself today
- ◯ I helped a friend in school

Keep up the awesome work!

What makes you scared?

1

2

3

How are you silly?

1

2

3

What makes you feel helpful?

1

2

3

Meet
The Happy Habits Club
Members

Centipede

Centipede is friends with Flip, Flop & Flo. He likes helping others.

Centipede

Sometimes Centipede gets scared. But then he remembers that being happy feels better.

Centipede laughs to make himself feel better.

What makes you laugh?

1

2

3

Keep up the awesome work!

Color Centipede

Beaver

Beaver is silly. He likes making his friends laugh and smile. Sometimes he feels like a clown.

Beaver

Beaver gets angry when his dam breaks and all the water washes down the stream.

But then he remembers that sometimes those things happen. He starts to laugh and build a new dam.

What do you think is funny?

1

2

3

Laugh really loud!

Color Beaver

Raccoon

Raccoon is nocturnal. She sleeps during the day and is awake at night. But when her friends need her, she's there for them.

She really likes taking naps!

Raccoon

Raccoon has the coolest dreams when she naps. She dreams of eating ice cream and cookies.

What do you dream of when you nap?

1

2

3

Sweet Dreams!

Color Raccoon

Can you draw
Mr. Gerry eating berries?

Can you draw yourself next to
the other animals?

Centipede   Beaver   Raccoon   You

Coloring Page

Coloring Page

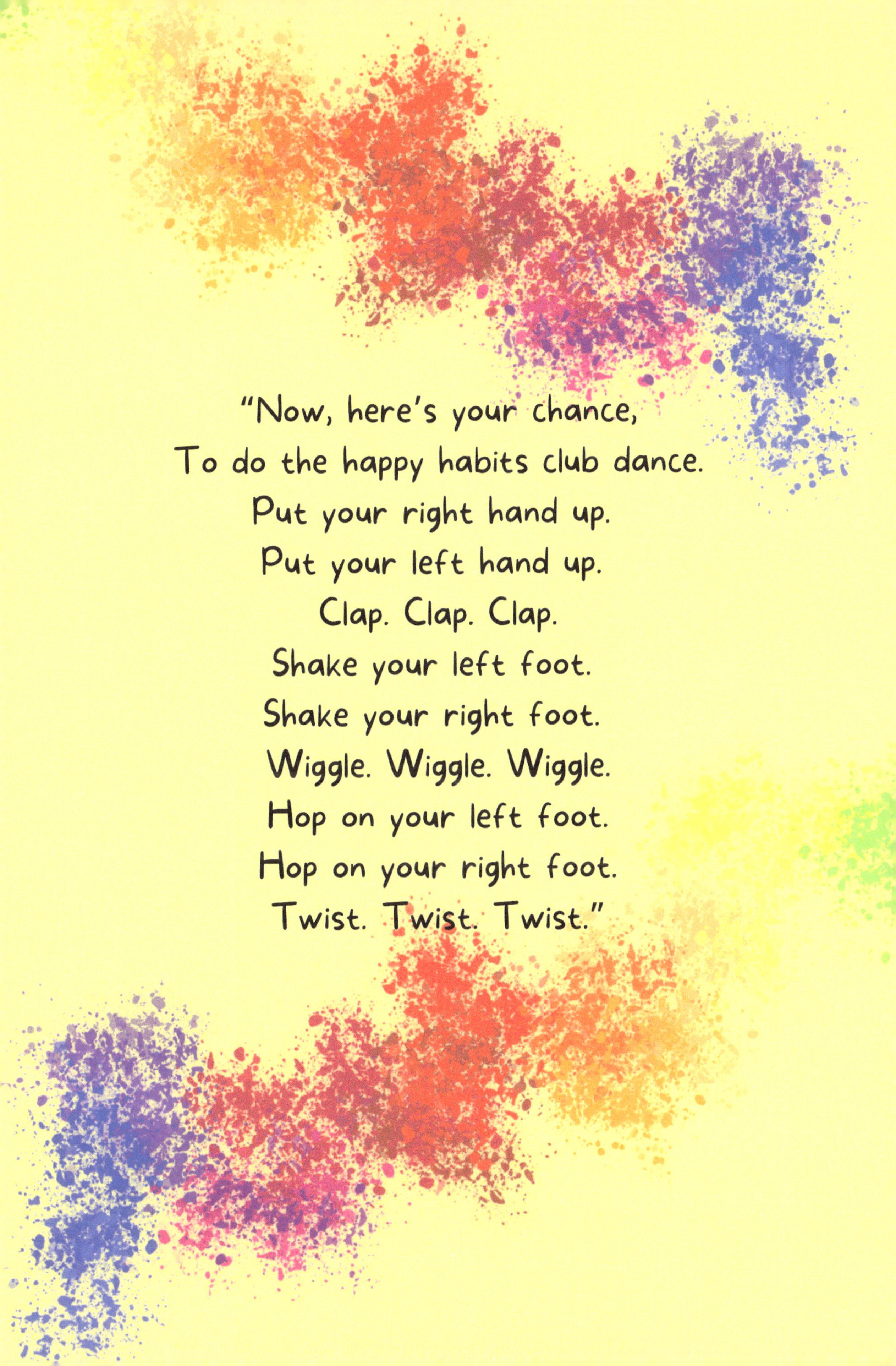

"Now, here's your chance,
To do the happy habits club dance.
Put your right hand up.
Put your left hand up.
Clap. Clap. Clap.
Shake your left foot.
Shake your right foot.
Wiggle. Wiggle. Wiggle.
Hop on your left foot.
Hop on your right foot.
Twist. Twist. Twist."

Happy Habits Club Books

The Happy Habits Club
Find Mrs. Mouse's Berries
Tank the Turtle Lost the Race
The Magic of Compliments
Mr. Grumplekins Discovers His Laugh

thehappyhabits.club

About the Author

Dr. Cheryl Robinson is a working model, an international speaker, founder of Creative Renegade Media & Ready2Roar and contributor for ForbesWomen with 27 Editors' Pick recognitions.

Having interviewed over 400 women and counting, she has had the fortunate opportunity to meet and engage with some of the most powerful, influential and inspiring women in the world, including Suzanne Shank, Kathleen Kennedy, Bobbi Brown, Diane von Furstenberg, Susie Wolff, Claire Williams, Christie Pearce Rampone, Maria Sharapova, La La Anthony, Melissa Rauch and Candace Cameron Bure.

As an international speaker, Cheryl has spoken, moderated and conducted workshops and panels for over 20 years. Her speaking portfolio includes engagements at Columbia University, Penn State, Columbia University/Oxbridge, Girl Meets World, Lakewood BlueClaws, the Acronis Women in Tech & Motorsports in Abu Dhabi and the U.N.'s Girl Up Teen Advisory Board.

Cheryl became a published author at the age of fourteen writing for the local newspaper. She's been published in multiple publications.

www.ingramcontent.com/pod-product-compliance
Lightning Source LLC
Chambersburg PA
CBHW042113030726
47599CB00002B/195